Junior Mini Mathematical Murder Mysteries

16 Activities to stretch and engage ages 8-11

Jill Whieldon

tarquin

Publisher's Note

This 'Junior' addition to Jill Whieldon's popular Mini Mathematical Murder Mystery Series allows primary pupils to join in the mystery solving fun.

You can keep up to date with this and other new titles, special offers and more, through registering on our website for our e-mail newsletter or following us on Twitter or Facebook.

Published by Tarquin Publications
Suite 74, 17 Holywell Hill
St Albans
AL1 1DT

www.tarquingroup.com

Copyright © Jill Whieldon, 2013
ISBN: 978-1-907550-81-2

Distributed in the USA by IPG
www.ipgbooks.com
www.amazon.com & major retailers

Distributed in Australia by OLM www.lat-olm.com.au

Printed in the USA and designed in the United Kingdom

16 Activities to stretch
and engage ages 8-11

Introduction

Here's a chance for students to turn detective and apply their mathematical knowledge to solve some murder mysteries.

For teachers

These are intended to be consolidation exercises covering arithmetic, algebra, shapes and simple graphs and charts. Students often work well in pairs on this sort of activity as they are able to discuss their methods and combine forces when coordinating several features of a problem. Some of the tasks require a reasonable level of logical thinking and students need to understand mathematical terms such as product, factor, prime, etc. The benefits to the students will be greatly improved if their knowledge of such mathematical language has been reinforced before attempting these murder mysteries. Success through this type of activity can increase student's confidence and make them eager to progress.

Some of the tasks included here reflect wider topics met in the primary school curriculum and there is an element of general knowledge evident.

Further investigative work could be generated from these, for example, in "Water": can you find a river whose length would fit between the Severn and the Thames?   In "Romans": can you find an emperor who reigned for less than 10 years?

I hope that your students will enjoy tackling these and that you will be able to gauge their understanding and application of basic mathematical skills through them.

For parents

Far more engaging than endless tests, these murder mysteries will use mathematical skills learnt at school to reinforce knowledge and stretch students who crave a challenge. Please ensure your child understands the concepts involved before you tackle the tasks as this will enable them to be successful.

I would strongly recommend talking about the mathematics involved with your child as this can help to improve explanations and methodology using appropriate mathematical language.

These exercises are intended to be entertaining, and I hope that your children enjoy using their mathematical skills to find out "whodunnit".

Jill Whieldon

Mini Murder Mystery
Mixed Arithmetic 1

WHO?

This addition table has some missing values. The 6 suspects have each made 2 statements about the numbers in the table. The murderer has made 2 incorrect statements and the victim has made no errors.

+	26	41	39	15
34	60	**A**	73	49
21	**B**	62	60	**C**
19	45	**D**	**E**	34
28	**F**	69	67	**G**

Phil said

- ❑ The missing number in position A is 75
- ❑ The total of the 4 answers in the "34" row is 247

Charlotte said

- ❑ The missing number at position E is 48
- ❑ The total of the 4 answers in the "39" column is 258

Danielle said

- ❑ Missing number B is 47
- ❑ The total of the 4 answers in the "21" row is 195

Josh said

- ❑ Missing number G is 9 less than missing number F
- ❑ The largest missing number is D

Scarlet said

- ❑ The sum of D and E is 118
- ❑ The smallest missing number is C

Samuel said

- ❑ F is 7 less than B
- ❑ The difference between B and C is 11

WHEN?

Here is a list of numbers in ascending order.

167, 178, 199, 289, 310, 455, 458, 475, 484

The hours part of the time is the difference between the highest even number and the highest odd number.	The minutes part of the time is the difference between the 2 lowest odd numbers.
The date of the murder is a tenth of the middle number.	The month is 4 times the smallest difference between numbers in the list.

Calendar icon: M T W T F S S

WHERE?

Write a list of the odd numbers between 20 and 30.

❏ If the sum of them is even, the murder happened at the theatre.	❏ If the sum of them is < 120, the murder happened at the cinema.
❏ If there are 2 multiples of 3 in the list, the murder happened at the literary festival.	❏ If the sum is > 130, the murder happened at the music festival.

WHY?

Calculate the following products then decode the murderer's confession.

A	B	D	E	H	I	L
2x3x4	10x3x5	2x3x3	3x4x5	8x1x4	2x2x10	3x6x2

M	N	O	R	S	U	
7x2x5	6x6x2	8x6x2	5x6x3	6x7x2	5x3x5	

84	32	60	84	24	40	18	18	96	75
150	36	60	24	72	96	18	18	72	75
70	150	60	90	40	84	96	18	18	

FINAL ACCUSATION

_____ murdered _____

At (time)_____ on (date) _____

At (where) _____

Because (why) _____

Mini Murder Mystery
Mixed Arithmetic 2

WHO?	The 6 suspects have each made 2 statements about the calculations shown here. The murderer has made 2 errors, the victim has made none.

(20 x 3) + (40 x 2)	500 ÷ (90 – 88)
(55 + 65) x 2	1000 – (1x 2 x3 x 4 x 5 x 6)
(73 x 4) – (16 x 12)	(99 x 2) – (3 x 2 x 13)

Hannah said
- ☐ The difference between the highest and lowest numbers is 180
- ☐ All the answers are even

Hepsibah said
- ☐ One pair of answers have a difference of 100
- ☐ The sum of the 2 highest answers is 490

Henrietta said
- ☐ All the answers are multiples of 10
- ☐ There is a difference of 10 between the 2 lowest numbers

Hercules said
- ☐ All the numbers are multiples of 20
- ☐ The total of all 6 answers is 1030

Henry said
- ☐ 2 answers are > 200 and 4 answers are < 200
- ☐ There is a difference of 30 between the 2 highest answers

Horatio said
- ☐ The product of the highest and lowest numbers is 25,000
- ☐ There are no odd numbers

WHEN?

Use these clues to work out the date and time of the murder.

Time: (in 24 hour, digital, like 12:46)	Date: (date and month, eg 30/8 is 30th Aug)
❏ All 4 digits are prime numbers and there are no repeats ❏ The 4 digits are in numerical order ❏ It is nearly midnight	❏ There are 3 digits, 2 for the day, 1 for the month ❏ Each digit is odd but not prime ❏ One digit is repeated ❏ The total of the digits is 11 ❏ The whole date is a palindrome

WHERE?

Decide whether these calculations are true or false. The letters will spell out the name of the place where the murder happened.

	If true choose this letter	If false choose this letter
$120 \div 4 = 90 \div 3$	M	B
$360 \div 18 = 1500 \div 750$	E	A
$425 \div 25 = 52 \div 3$	T	R
$864 \div 4 = 54 \times 4$	K	E
$2000 \div 50 = 1600 \div 4$	R	E
$780 \div 2 \div 2 = 38 \times 5$	N	T

WHY?

Work out the answers to these negative number calculations, then decode the message.

A	B	D	E	H	I	M
$-12 + 4$	$-6 + 8$	$-12 + 2$	$-4 - 12$	$-6 - 5$	$-4 - 8$	$-5 + 6$

N	O	P	R	S	U	W
$-8 - 6$	$4 - 8$	$-4 + 12$	$-8 + 6$	$8 - 4$	$-6 + 5$	$-2 - 4$

4	-11	-16	4	-8	-12	-10	-4	-14	-16	-6	-8	

4	-8	8	-2	-12	1	-16	-14	-1	1	2	-16	-2

FINAL ACCUSATION

_____ murdered _____

At (time)_____ on (date) _____

At (where) _____

Because (why) _____

Mini Murder Mystery Number & Algebra 1

WHO?

The 6 suspects have each made 2 statements about the books and authors shown here.
The murderer has made 2 errors, the victim has made none.

	Sums U Like	The Shape of Things to Come	A for Arithmetic	Symmetry Through the Looking Glass	My Best Friend χ
author's age	45	37	20	55	73
weight of book	270g	0.25kg	135g	1.35kg	300g
no. of pages	320	220	100	400	270
publication date	30/4/12	10/12/11	21/1/12	19/8/12	11/11/11

Lisa said
- ☐ The oldest author is 73
- ☐ The lightest book is only 25g

Matt said
- ☐ The 2nd youngest author wrote Sums U Like
- ☐ The thickest book has 4 times the number of pages of the thinnest book.

Joshua said
- ☐ Symmetry Through the Looking Glass is the thickest book
- ☐ The book published in April is Sums U Like

Gloria said
- ☐ The book with the most words in its title is the heaviest
- ☐ A for Arithmetic is the lightest book

Mary-Jane said
- ☐ The book published in January weighs a quarter of a kilogram.
- ☐ Only 1 book has over 300 pages

Isaac said
- ☐ The book published in November is by the oldest author
- ☐ The symmetry book and the arithmetic book weigh the same.

WHEN?

You have to work out the time of the murder.
It was in the morning.

:

The angle between the hour hand and minute hand is exactly 60°
The minute hand is pointing to 12
Written in digital format, the time has a horizontal line of symmetry

WHERE?

Check these sums. Some are true and some are false. Link the number of true statements to the place of the murder.

24 + 19 = 50 - 7
56 – 16 = 23 + 27
8 x 4 = 2 x 2 x 2 x 2 x 2
120 ÷ 24 = 30 – 9 - 16
½ of 38 = 6 x 3

If all 5 are true it happened in Kent	If just 4 are true it happened in Devon	If just 3 are true it happened in Yorkshire	If just 2 are true it happened in Durham

WHY?

The murderer has made a statement. Calculate the missing value in each equation to decode the confession.

A	D	E	H	I	N
□ + 3 = 12	? – 12 = 8	4 x ✳ = 20	40 - ◆ = 22	36 ÷ ✖ = 12	◪ + ◪ = 12
O	R	S	T	W	
★ x 9 = 9	24 ÷ ◀ = 2	3x▲+▲ = 8	⦿ ÷ 3 = 5	3 x ◈ = 30	

18	5	20	3	20	6	1	15	10
5	9	12	18	3	2	18	9	15

FINAL ACCUSATION

_____ murdered _____

At (time) _____

At (where) _____

Because (why) _____

Mini Murder Mystery
Number and Algebra 2

WHO? Each of these children has a favourite 3 digit number under 200 and has made 3 statements about it.
You have to work out what their favourite numbers are.

They then stand in a line lowest to highest.

The person at the highest end of the line has murdered the one at the lowest end.

Chloe said

- ❑ My number is an exact power of 2
- ❑ It is 3 higher than a cube number
- ❑ There are 2 people between me and Billy

Macey said

- ❑ My number is a multiple of 11
- ❑ The sum of its digits is 8
- ❑ Chloe is next but 1 to me

Dean said

- ❑ I am standing next to Chloe
- ❑ My number is a multiple of 12
- ❑ My number is 12 less than a square number

Aisha said

- ❑ I am standing between Bradley and Chloe
- ❑ My number is under 120
- ❑ It is a multiple of 5

Billy said

- ❑ My number is a square number
- ❑ I am standing next to Bradley
- ❑ The product of my digits is 0

Bradley said

- ❑ There are 2 people between me and Dean
- ❑ My number is a multiple of 3
- ❑ The product of the digits is 1

WHEN?

Use the substitutions a=1, b=2, c=3, … y=25, z=26 to work out these answers.

The date of the murder was $3w - 4j$	The month of the murder was $2m - r$
The hour part of the time was $(ft \div ce) \times b$	The minutes part of the time was $kh \div ab$

WHERE?

Here are 4 worded calculations.
Work them all out then decide where the murder took place.

⅓ of the number of days in November times ⅔ of the number of days in November	The product of 2 cubed and 5 squared	The difference between 3x400 and 5x200	The sum of the first 20 whole numbers

In a plane if all of the answers are 200	In a hot air balloon if 3 answers are 200
In a glider if 2 of the answers are 200	In a spaceship if only 1 answer is 200

WHY?

Solve the equations then decode the murderer's confession.

A	E	G	H	I	K	L
$4A = 20$	$3+ E = 10$	$12- G = 3$	$H - 10 = 7$	$6I = 36$	$2k = 32$	$6 + L = 14$
N	O	P	R	S	T	V
$N \div 4 = 8$	$10 \div O = 5$	$15 - P = 3$	$20 - R = 7$	$2S = 30$	$T \div 10 = 5$	$5V = 5$

17	7	32	7	1	7	13	15	50	2
12	15	50	5	8	16	6	32	9	

FINAL ACCUSATION

_____ murdered _____

At (time)_____ on (date) _____

At (where) _____

Because (why) _____

Mini Murder Mystery
Number and Angle Mix

WHO?

Each of the children has chosen a different number from 20 to 30. Each has made 3 statements about their number. The murderer has chosen the highest number, the victim the lowest.

Rob said

- ❑ My number is even
- ❑ It has 2 pairs of factors
- ❑ It is a factor of 208

Fiona said

- ❑ My number is the product of the first 3 prime numbers
- ❑ It is even
- ❑ It is a factor of 360

Lisa said

- ❑ My number is prime
- ❑ It is higher than Colin's number
- ❑ It is a factor of 232

Claire said

- ❑ My number is odd
- ❑ It is a cube number
- ❑ It is a multiple of 9

Tony said

- ❑ My number is even
- ❑ It has 4 pairs of factors
- ❑ It is a factor of 360

Colin said

- ❑ My number is odd
- ❑ It only has 3 factors
- ❑ It is a square number

WHEN?

Work out the next term for each of these 3 sequences. Then add the 3 answers together. Then link your total to the day of the murder.

36, 45, 54, _____	900, 750, 600, _____	28, 18, 8, _____
3 days ago if the total is 611		The day before yesterday if the total is 605
Yesterday if the total is 505		Today if the total is 511

WHERE?

Calculate the missing angle in these 4 shapes. Then add the answers together and link the total to the place where the murder happened.

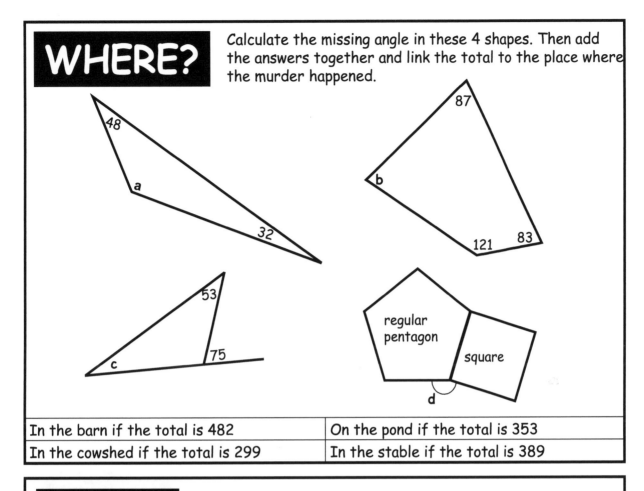

In the barn if the total is 482	On the pond if the total is 353
In the cowshed if the total is 299	In the stable if the total is 389

WHY?

Work out these % calculations then decode the murderer's reason.

A	B	E		G	H
12% of 450	12½% of 360	125% of 360		20% of 360	90% of 360
K	L	O	R	S	T
90% of 450	150% of 360	10% of 360	25% of 360	45% of 360	40% of 360

324	450	45	90	36	405	450	54	540
540	144	324	450	450	72	72	162	

FINAL ACCUSATION

_____ murdered _____

When _____

At (where) _____

Because (why) _____

Mini Murder Mystery
Money

   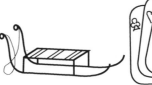

WHO?

The 6 people below have each bought 1 item in a sale. They have each made 2 statements. The person who made 2 false statements has murdered the person who made 2 true statements. Work out the murderer and the victim.

Was £4.60 Now half price	Was £10.50 £2.20 off in the sale	Was £15 ⅓ off in the sale	Was £8.20 Now 25% off	Was £2.90 You pay 50%	Was £19.50 £9.90 off in the sale

Albert said
- ❏ I bought a football and it cost me £8.30
- ❏ The sledge only costs £2.05

Bryony said
- ❏ The teddy is the most expensive sale item
- ❏ I spent £2.30 on the bucket and spade

Dylan said
- ❏ The doll costs £5 in the sale
- ❏ I bought the playing cards and received 65p change from a £2 coin

Will said
- ❏ I bought the teddy and received 40p change from a £10 note
- ❏ The saving on the sledge is £2.50

Elspeth said
- ❏ I bought the cards and paid the correct amount with 2 50p coins, 2 20p coins, 2 2p coins and a 1p coin
- ❏ The teddy is reduced to less than half price

Matthew said
- ❏ The teddy was most expensive before and during the sale
- ❏ In the sale the bucket and spade cost £6 less than the football

WHEN?

❑ If double £5.60 is £10.20 the date of the murder was Oct 20th	❑ If double £4.55 is £9.10 the murder was on 10th September
❑ If double £5.09 is £11.18 the murder was on 18th November	❑ If double £6.05 is £12.01 the murder was on the 1st December

❑ If half of £25.40 is £12.40 the time of the murder was 12:40	❑ If half of £31.30 is £15.15, then the time of the murder was 15:15
❑ If half of £13.06 is £6.53 the murder happened at 06:53	❑ If half of £35.50 is £17.25 the murder happened at 17:25

WHERE?

Add all these prices together:

46p, £12.90, 8p, £6.40, 325p, £2.91

❑ In the toyshop if the total is £24	❑ In the library if the total is £25
❑ In the leisure centre if the total is £26	❑ In the café if the total is £27

WHY?

Calculate the change from £5 for each of these totals. Then decode the murderer's confession.

A	C	E	G	H	M	N
£3.50	£1.99	£2.75	£2.15	90p	£0.75	£3.99
O	R	S	T	V	W	
£1.25	£1.90	£1.85	£3.35	£2.40	£2.35	

£3.15	£4.10	£2.25	£2.85	£1.50	£2.60	£2.25	£4.25
£2.25	£1.65	£4.10	£2.25	£2.65	£3.10	£3.75	£1.01
£2.85	£3.01	£4.10	£1.50	£1.01	£2.85	£2.25	

FINAL ACCUSATION

_____ murdered _____

At (time)_____ on (date) _____

At (where) _____

Because (why) _____

Mini Murder Mystery
Coordinates

WHO? The grid below has 4 squares drawn on, but each is missing its 4th corner. The 6 suspects have each stated what they think the missing coordinates should be. The murderer has got them all wrong, the victim has got them all correct.

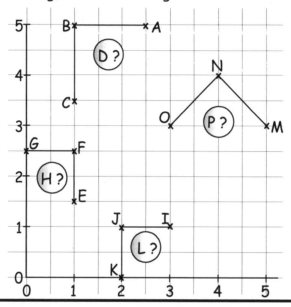

Susanna said
- ❑ D is (3.5 , 2.5)
- ❑ H is (1.5 , 0)
- ❑ L is (0 , 3)
- ❑ P is (2 , 4)

Hajira said
- ❑ D is (3.5 , 2.5)
- ❑ H is (0 , 1.5)
- ❑ L is (3 , 0)
- ❑ P is (2 , 4)

Ollie said
- ❑ D is (2.5 , 3.5)
- ❑ H is (0 , 1.5)
- ❑ L is (3 , 0)
- ❑ P is (2 , 4)

Ingrid said
- ❑ D is (3.5 , 2.5)
- ❑ H is (1.5 , 0)
- ❑ L is (3 , 0)
- ❑ P is (4 , 2)

Felix said
- ❑ D is (2.5, 3.5)
- ❑ H is (0 , 1.5)
- ❑ L is (3 , 0)
- ❑ P is (4 , 2)

Jerome said
- ❑ D is (2.5, 3.5)
- ❑ H is (1.5, 0)
- ❑ L is (3 , 0)
- ❑ P is (4 , 2)

Coordinates – Student Sheet 1

WHEN?

❑ The hours part of the time is the length of a line from (2,7) to (12,7)	❑ The minutes part of the time is the length of a line from (5,10) to (25,10)
❑ The date of the murder is the length of a line from (18,21) to (39,21)	❑ The month of the murder is the length of a line from (30,5) to (30,7)

WHERE?

Continue the 3 lines in their given directions. They will enclose a triangle. In the triangle are some coordinates. The murder happened at the only point inside the triangle where both coordinates are whole numbers.

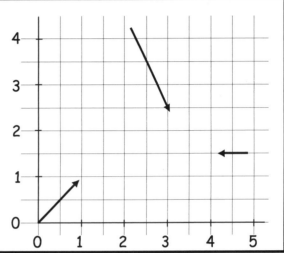

WHY?

Work out the coordinates of the point that is...

A	D	E	H	I	L	N
2 above (1,3)	3 below (5,3)	1 above (4,4)	1 above (0,2)	1 left of (3,2)	2 left of (4,3)	2 right of (3,3)
O	P	R	S	T	V	
3 below (3,3)	2 right of (2,1)	2 below (3,5)	2 above (4,2)	1 right of (2,2)	1 right of (2,1)	

(0,3)	(4,5)	(4,1)	(2,3)	(3,0)	(3,2)	(3,2)	(4,5)	(5,0)	(1,5)	(4,1)	(3,0)

(2,2)	(5,3)	(3,2)	(2,2)	(5,3)	(3,3)	(4,5)	(3,1)	(4,5)	(3,3)	(4,4)	(4,5)

FINAL ACCUSATION

_____ murdered _____

At (time)_____ on (date) _____

At (where) _____

Because (why) _____

Mini Murder Mystery
Shape

WHO? The 6 suspects below have all made 2 statements about the areas of these shapes. The murderer has made 2 errors, the victim has made none.

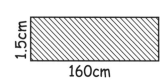
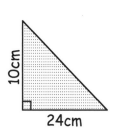

1.5cm
160cm

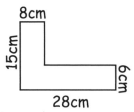
8cm
15cm
6cm
28cm

16cm
16cm

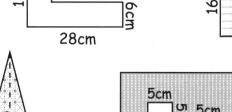
10cm
24cm

20cm
18cm

5cm
5cm
5cm
5cm
16cm
20cm

Alexandra said
☐ The right angled triangle has the smallest area
☐ The square has the largest area

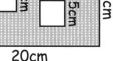

Jenny said
☐ The shape with 2 holes in has an area of 300cm²
☐ One triangle is double the other

Caius said
☐ The "L" has an area of 288cm²
☐ The rectangle is double the right angled triangle

Rosie said
☐ The isosceles triangle is 60cm² less than the rectangle
☐ The square's area is 64cm²

Harrison said
☐ The right angled triangle is 60cm² more than the isosceles triangle
☐ The rectangle and the "L" have equal areas

Oscar said
☐ The isosceles triangle is 1.5 times the right angled triangle
☐ The square is 16cm² more than the rectangle

Shape – Student Sheet 1

WHEN?

- The hours part of the time is the perimeter of a square whose edges each measure 4.5cm
- The minutes part of the time is the perimeter of a rectangle that measures 5.5cm by 8cm.
- The date of the murder is the perimeter of a rhombus whose edges each measure 5cm.
- The month of the murder is the perimeter of a regular hexagon whose edges each measure 1.5cm

WHERE?

Here are 4 road names. Decide which statement is true to find the place of the murder.

PARK WAY
Every letter has just 1 line of symmetry

LITTLE LANE
All the vowels have at least 1 line of symmetry

TEMPLE RIDE
All the consonants have a line of symmetry

HIGH STREET
Every letter has a line of symmetry

WHY?

Work out the missing height for a triangle to make an area of 36cm^2 and decode the murderer's confession.

A	D	E	F	H
Base =12cm	Base = 6cm	Base = 9cm	Base = 18cm	Base = 36cm
I	K	S	T	V
Base = 2 cm	Base = 10cm	Base = 1cm	Base = 4cm	Base = 3cm

2	8	72	6	36	12	6	7.2	36	18	8	2
6	12	4	36	24	8	72	36	12	8	72	

FINAL ACCUSATION

_____ murdered _____

At (time)_____ on (date) _____

At (where) _____

Because (why) _____

Mini Murder Mystery Charts

WHO?

60 pupils were asked which of these 5 vegetables was their favourite. The results were split into girls and boys.
The 6 suspects in a murder have each made 2 statements about the bar charts. The murderer has made 2 errors, the victim none.

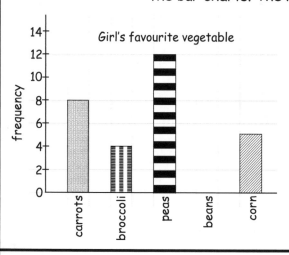

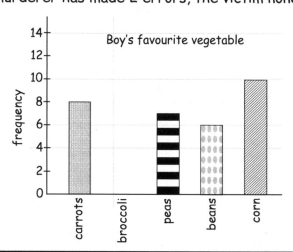

Petra said

☐ There are 30 girls and 30 boys

☐ The same number of girls and boys chose carrots

Bonnie said

☐ More boys chose corn than girls

☐ There are less boys

Fred said

☐ Twice as many girls chose carrots as broccoli

☐ No boys chose broccoli

Monika said

☐ Twice as many girls chose corn as boys

☐ The most popular vegetable overall was peas

Toby said

☐ There are 31 girls and 29 boys

☐ $6\frac{1}{2}$ boys chose peas

Simon said

☐ There are 2 more boys than girls

☐ There are 14 girls

WHEN?

Look back at the bar charts for these.

- ❑ The hours part of the time is the number of girls who chose peas
- ❑ The minutes part of the time is the total number of girls
- ❑ The date is the total number of boys who chose peas and carrots
- ❑ The month is the number of boys who chose corn

WHERE?

62 lottery winners were asked what the first thing they did with some of their money was.

Their answers are in the tally chart, but some numbers are missing. Work out the 5 missing values and match your answers with the place of the murder. If they are ...

	tally	frequency
buy a new house	ⅼⱵⱵ ⅼⱵⱵ ⅼⅼⅼ	A
go on a holiday	ⅼⱵⱵ ⅼⱵⱵ ⅼⱵⱵ ⅼⱵⱵ ⅼⅼⅼ	B
give some to charity	C	13
save it all	D	E

A=13	A=18	A=15	A=18
B=23	B=23	B=23	B=23
C= ⅼⱵⱵ ⅼⱵⱵ ⅼⅼⅼ	C= ⅼⱵⱵ ⅼⱵⱵ ⅼⅼⅼ	C= ⅼⱵⱵ ⅼⱵⱵ ⅼⅼⅼ	C= ⅼⱵⱵ ⅼⱵⱵ ⅼⱵⱵ ⅼⅼⅼ
D= ⅼⱵⱵ ⅼⱵⱵ ⅼⅼⅼ	D= ⅼⱵⱵ ⅼⅼⅼ	D= ⅼⱵⱵ ⅼⱵⱵ	D= ⅼⱵⱵ ⅼⅼⅼ
E=13	E=8	E=10	E=8
In the pantry	In the utility room	In the scullery	In the wash room

WHY?

Starting with A=1, use substitution to work out the values of the other letters to decode the murderer's confession.

A	D	E	F	H	I
1	S + A	2 x D	5 x i	P - D	U - T
P	R	S	T	U	
T - A	F ÷ 2	3 x A	D + E	2 x H	

7	8	3	1	2	4	1	11	8

1	2	3	1	10	5	14	2	12

FINAL ACCUSATION

_____ murdered _____

At (time)_____ on (date) _____

At (where) _____

Because (why) _____

Mini Murder Mystery Family

WHO?

Here are some facts about the 6 suspects and their brothers and sisters. Read the 6 statements underneath and decide whether they are true or false.

Jane	Julie	Jill	John	Jack	James
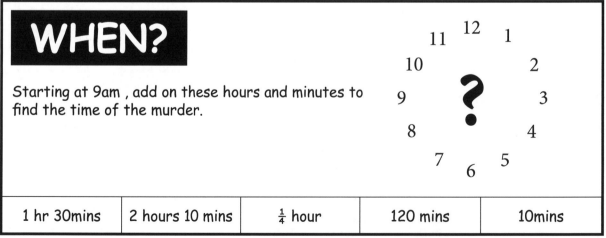					
I have ... 2 brothers 0 sisters	I have ... 1 brother 1 sister	I have ... 0 brothers 1 sister	I have ... 2 brothers 1 sister	I have ... 0 brothers 0 sisters	I have ... 2 brothers 0 sisters

Jane, John and James each have 2 brothers	True or False?	❑
There are 2 families with 3 children	True or False?	❑
There is just 1 family with no sons	True or False?	❑
John's sister has 3 brothers	True or False?	❑
James's family is the only one with no daughters	True or False?	❑

❑ If 5 statements are true, Jane is the murderer ❑ If 4 statements are true, Julie is the murderer ❑ If 3 statements are true, Jill is the murderer	The victim has the same number of letters in their name as the murderer and the same number of brothers as the murderer

WHEN?

Starting at 9am , add on these hours and minutes to find the time of the murder.

11 12 1
10 2
9 **?** 3
8 4
7 5
6

1 hr 30mins	2 hours 10 mins	$\frac{1}{4}$ hour	120 mins	10mins

WHERE?

Write these numbers in digits then find the correct combination below.

two million four hundred and sixty eight thousand eight hundred and fifty six
one million sixty thousand three hundred and thirty
five million four thousand and twenty two

	At a wishing well if the numbers are:	2 468 856	1 060 330	5 422
	At the top of a hill if the numbers are:	2 468 856	160 330	5 004 022
	At the bottom of a hill if the numbers are:	2 468 856	1 060 330	5 004 022
	At home if the numbers are:	2 468 856	1 006 330	5 400 022

WHY?

Calculate these 2 and 3 times table answers to decode the murderer's confession.

A	D	E	H	I
26 × 2	15 × 3	13 × 3	16 × 2	18 × 3
L	M	N	O	P
21 × 3	33 × 2	19 × 3	17 × 2	25 × 3
S	T	U	W	
24 × 2	35 × 2	34 × 3	19 × 2	

38	39	38	39	57	70	102	75	52	32
54	63	63	52	57	45	32	39	75	102
48	32	39	45	66	39	45	34	38	57

FINAL ACCUSATION

_____ murdered _____

At (time) _____

At (where) _____

Because (why) _____

Mini Murder Mystery
Sports

WHO? Each of 6 students has made 3 statements about their results in 3 individual sportevents. Fill in the gaps in this table from their information. The murderer was the 2nd fastest runner and the victim is the person whose positions add up to the lowest number.

	100m position	100m time	long jump position	long jump distance	weight lifting position	weight lifted
Sidney				4.30m	2nd	
Brooklyn			2nd			
Cassandra	5th		5th		4th	
Evie						
Thomas		12.8 sec				
Murtada				4.11m		18.750kg

Sidney said

- [ ] I came 4th in the 100m, 0.2sec slower than Evie
- [ ] My best position was in weightlifting. I lifted 20.25kg
- [ ] I came 3rd in long jump, 1.3m behind the winner, Thomas

Cassandra said

- [ ] I beat Brooklyn by 3 secs in the 100m. I took 18.9sec
- [ ] I jumped 4.01m
- [ ] I lifted 4kg more than Evie, but 4kg less than Sidney

Brooklyn said

- [ ] I won the weightlifting with double Evie's lift
- [ ] I came last in 1 event
- [ ] I jumped 5.2m

Evie said

- [ ] I was last in long jump, 36cm less than Cassandra
- [ ] I ran the 100m in 14.4 sec. Only Thomas and Murtada were faster
- [ ] I was 5th in weightlifting

Thomas said

- [ ] I won 2 events and came last in the other.
- [ ] I jumped 40cm further than Brooklyn
- [ ] I lifted 14kg less than Brooklyn

Murtada said

- [ ] I came 2nd, 3rd and 4th in the events.
- [ ] I was 0.3 sec faster than Sidney in the 100m
- [ ] I jumped 10cm further than Cassandra

WHERE?

Here are the results of a football tournament between 4 schools. Put them in descending order of the number of goals scored to find out where the murder happened.

Briarfoot 6 – Compton Rd 2	If it is Park Lane, Compton Rd, Briarfoot, St Martins then the murder happened at St Martins School.
Compton Rd 2 – St Martins 2	
Park Lane 1 – Briarfoot 0	If it is St Martins, Compton Rd, Briarfoot, Park Lane, then the murder happened at Park Lane School.
St Martins 4 – Park Lane 2	If it is Compton Rd, St Martins, Park Lane, Briarfoot, then the murder happened at Briarfoot School.
Briarfoot 3 – St Martins 4	
Compton Rd 4 – Park Lane 3	If it is St Martins, Briarfoot, Compton Rd, Park Lane, then the murder happened at Compton Rd School.

WHEN?

- ☐ The hours part of the time is the total number of goals scored by Compton Rd and Park Lane.
- ☐ The minutes part of the time is the total goals scored by all the schools.
- ☐ The date of the crime is the difference between the total goals of Compton Rd and Park Lane.
- ☐ The month of the crime is half the number of goals scored by St Martins.

WHY?

Change these times into seconds to decode the murderer's confession.

A	C	D	E	G	H	I
2 mins	$\frac{3}{4}$ min	2.5 mins	1.5 mins	3 mins	1min 50sec	$1\frac{2}{3}$ mins
N	O	R	T	U	W	
$3\frac{1}{3}$ mins	1.25mins	1min 25 sec	$\frac{1}{2}$ min	1min 10 sec	$\frac{1}{100}$ hour	

100	36	120	200	30	90	150	30	75
36	100	200	30	110	90	85	70	200
200	100	200	180	85	120	45	90	

FINAL ACCUSATION

_____ murdered _____

At (time)_____ on (date) _____

At (where) _____

Because (why) _____

Mini Murder Mystery Music

WHO?

The 6 suspects have each made 2 statements about the songs in this table. The murderer has made 2 errors, the victim has made none.

Title	Length	Number Sold	Date Released
Come Back	3min 40sec	200 000	Apr 2011
Doopy Do Dah	4min 25sec	375 000	Aug 2012
Welcome to Here	3min 55sec	295 000	Dec 2012
Don't Do That	2min 50sec	185 000	Feb 2013
Heaven is the House Next Door	4min 5sec	145 000	Apr 2013

Clara said
- The song with the longest title sold the least.
- The song released first was the longest

Kate said
- Don't Do That was 1min 10 sec shorter than Come Back
- The song released 3rd was the 2nd best seller

Benjie said
- The 2 songs released in 2013 didn't sell as many in total as Doopy Do Dah
- The 2nd longest song sold least

Jonnie said
- The 2nd shortest song sold 295 000 copies
- Welcome to Here was the middle length song

Kyle said
- The song released 2nd sold the most copies
- The December song lasted over 4mins

Georgina said
- The shortest song sold the least
- The August release had the shortest title

WHEN?

Here is a calendar page for March one year. Follow these instructions to work out the murder date.

			MARCH			
SUN	MON	TUES	WED	THUR	FRI	SAT
		1	2	3	4	5
6	7	8	9	10	11	12
13	14	15	16	17	18	19
20	21	22	23	24	25	26
27	28	29	30	31		

- Start on March 12th.
- In a fortnight's time it will be ....
- 3 days before that is ....
- In a week's time it will be .... – the murder day!

WHERE?

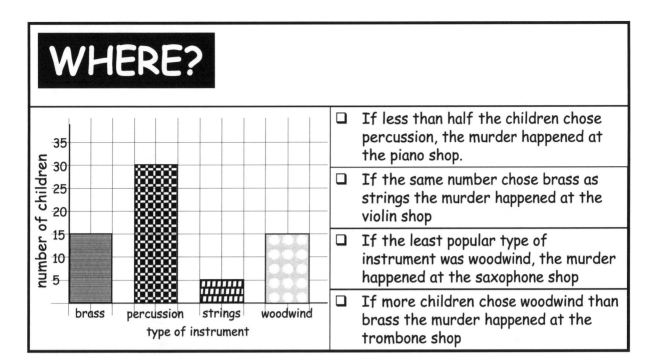

☐ If less than half the children chose percussion, the murder happened at the piano shop.

☐ If the same number chose brass as strings the murder happened at the violin shop

☐ If the least popular type of instrument was woodwind, the murder happened at the saxophone shop

☐ If more children chose woodwind than brass the murder happened at the trombone shop

WHY?

Work out the total for each letter then decode the murderer's confession.

$W = 4$ $H = 2$ $q = 1$ $e = \frac{1}{2}$ $X = \frac{1}{4}$

A	B	C	E	H	I	L
w H	H q	H e	w x q	w x	q x	q

N	O	P	S	T	U	Y
e H x	w e	q ex	x x	H H	H x	e x

3	5¼	2½	6	2¼	½	5¼	4¼	5¼	2½	6	2¾	4

1¾	1	6	¾	4	4¼	5¼	1¾	1¼	6	2¾	4½	

FINAL ACCUSATION

_____ murdered _____

On (date) _____

At (where) _____

Because (why) _____

Mini Murder Mystery
Europe

WHO?

The 6 suspects have each made 2 statements about the countries in this table.
The murderer has made 2 errors, the victim has made none.

	height of highest mountain	length of coastline	population	capital
France	4 810 m	4 853 km	65 400 000	Paris
Germany	2 962 m	2 389 km	81 726 000	Berlin
Norway	2 469 m	25 148 km	4 952 000	Oslo
Poland	2 655 m	440 km	38 216 000	Warsaw
Greece	2 917 m	13 676 km	11 300 000	Athens

Gillian said

- ❑ The country whose capital has an odd number of letters has the 2ⁿᵈ biggest population
- ❑ Greece has the 2ⁿᵈ longest coastline

Jodie said

- ❑ Norway has the smallest high mountain and the smallest population
- ❑ The highest mountain is more than double the smallest

Jasmine saids

- ❑ The country with the 2ⁿᵈ highest mountain has a capital with an odd number of letters.
- ❑ 2 countries have the same number of letters as their capitals

Jasper said

- ❑ The country whose capital has the least letters has the longest coastline
- ❑ The highest mountain is in the country with the highest population

Jack said

- ❑ The country with the shortest coastline has the smallest high mountain
- ❑ Greece's population is more than double Poland's

Joey said

- ❑ The difference between France's and Germany's population is over 20 million
- ❑ Norway's coastline is longer than all the others added together

WHEN?

❑ Finland is 2 hours ahead of UK time.
The murder happened when the time in Finland was 19:35. What time was it in the UK ?

❑ The Patron Saint of Germany is St Boniface. His special day is June 5th.
The murder happened 100 days after this. What date is that ?

WHERE?

This is a map of a journey through some countries in Europe, starting in Turkey and finishing in Spain. Which set of directions is correct ?

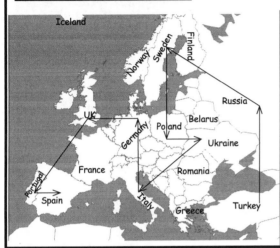

❑ The murder happened in Romania if the directions are
N, NW, S, W, SW, N, E, SW, E

❑ The murder happened in France if the directions are
N, NW, S, E, SW, N, E, SE, E

❑ The murder happened in Belarus if the directions are
N, NW, S, E, SW, N, W, SW, E

❑ The murder happened in Greece if the directions are
N, NE, S, W, SE, N, E, SE, W

WHY?

Different countries use different currencies. Convert these amounts into £s to decode the murderer's confession.

£1 = 8.80 Danish Krone(DK)   £1 = 1.20 Euros(€)   £1 = 4.90 Polish Zloty(Z)

A	D	E	H	I	J	M
17.60 DK	13.20 DK	19.60 Z	24€	49Z	147 Z	9.60 €
N	O	R	S	T	W	
14.40 €	220 DK	18€	68.60 Z	13.2 €	4.40 DK	

£20	£4	£15	£12	£2	£8	£4	£1.50	£25	£4	£14	£12

£11	£14	£11	£2	£15	£11	£0.50	£10	£11	£20	£2	£30

FINAL ACCUSATION

_____ murdered _____

At (time)_____ on (date) _____

At (where) _____

Because (why) _____

Mini Murder Mystery
The Romans

 **WHO?** Here is a table with details of 5 Roman emperors.
The 6 suspects have each made 2 statements about the emperors. The murderer has made 2 errors, the victim none.

name	born in	length of time as emperor	how they died
Augustus	63BC	40yrs 7mths	natural causes
Tiberius	42BC	22yrs 6mths	assassinated
Caligula	12AD	3yrs 10mths	assassinated
Claudius	10BC	13yrs 9mths	poisoned
Nero	37AD	13yrs 8mths	suicide

Julius said

☐ The emperor who was poisoned was born 3rd

☐ Caligula had the shortest reign as emperor

Maximus said

☐ The total reign of the 2 assassinated emperors was 26 years and 4 months

☐ Claudius reigned 1 month less than Nero

Hadrian said

☐ Tiberius was born before Augustus

☐ The emperor born last committed suicide

Juno said

☐ Caligula was born 2 years after Claudius

☐ The difference between the longest and shortest reigns is 37 years and 3 months

Chrysanta said

☐ The emperor who was born 2nd was assassinated

☐ The emperor who died naturally reigned for 47 months

Ligea said

☐ The emperor who reigned for 164 months was poisoned

☐ The 2 emperors born after the birth of Christ reigned for 17 years and 6 months in total

WHEN?

A large mosaic is made by copying this set of 16 coloured tiles 4 times.

The hours part of the time is the number of black tiles that will be needed in total.	The minutes part of the time is the total number of white tiles needed.
The date of the murder is the total number of grey tiles needed	The month of the murder is the difference between the total number of white tiles and the total number of black tiles.

WHERE?

Using the approximate breakdown shown, work out how many soldiers make up an army.

An army = 30 legions   A legion = 10 cohorts   A cohort = 6 troops   1 troop = 80 soldiers

❑ At Pompeii in Italy if it's 14 400	❑ At Hadrian's Wall in England if it's 48 000
❑ At Leptis Magna in Libya if it's 144 000	❑ At Segovia's Aqueduct in Spain if it's 1 440 000

WHY?

Convert these into Roman Numerals to decode the murderer's confession.

A	D	E	H	I	M
111	25	9	33	5	55
N	O	R	S	T	Y
19	7	91	1001	500	122

XXXIII	V	MI	LV	VII	XIX	D	XXXIII	XXXIII

CXI	MI	CXI	XXV	CXI	CXXII	LV	VII	XCI

IX	D	XXXIII	CXI	XIX	LV	V	XIX	IX

FINAL ACCUSATION

_____ murdered _____

At (time)_____ on (date) _____

At (where) _____

Because (why) _____

Mini Murder Mystery
Water

WHO?

The 6 suspects have each made 3 statements about the lengths of the rivers in this table (all in miles). The murderer has made 2 errors, the victim has made none.

River Thames 215   River Nile 4132   River Severn 220

River Amazon 3976   Mekong River 2705   River Don 1162

River Loire 629   Colorado River 824   Murray-Darling 2282

Darlene said

☐ The Nile is the longest

☐ The Loire is longer than the Colorado

Brendan said

☐ The Murray-Darling is the 4th longest

☐ The Amazon is more than 1200miles longer than the Mekong

Colin said

☐ If you add the Don and the Mekong together, it's longer than the Amazon

☐ The Thames is the shortest

Pippa said

☐ 5 times the Colorado is longer than the Nile.

☐ The Nile is 156 miles longer than the Amazon

Tommy said

☐ If you add the Thames and the Severn it's longer than the Nile.

☐ The Murray-Darling is 523 miles shorter than the Mekong

Louise says

☐ The Mekong is more than 10 times as long as the Severn

☐ The Thames, Loire and Severn are longer in total than the Don

WHEN?

A large tank of water is full and holds 60 litres.
A bucket and jug are used to empty it.
The bucket holds 9 litres.
The jug holds 1.5 litres.

9l   1.5l

If it can be emptied with 6 buckets and 2 jugs the crime happened at 5:12pm	If it can be emptied with 4 buckets and 14 jugs the crime happened at 4:14pm
If it can be emptied with 5 buckets and 10 jugs the crime happened at 5:10pm	If it can be emptied with 4 buckets and 12 jugs the crime happened at 4:12pm

WHERE?

Here are 4 containers. Put them in ascending order of volume to find out where the murder happened

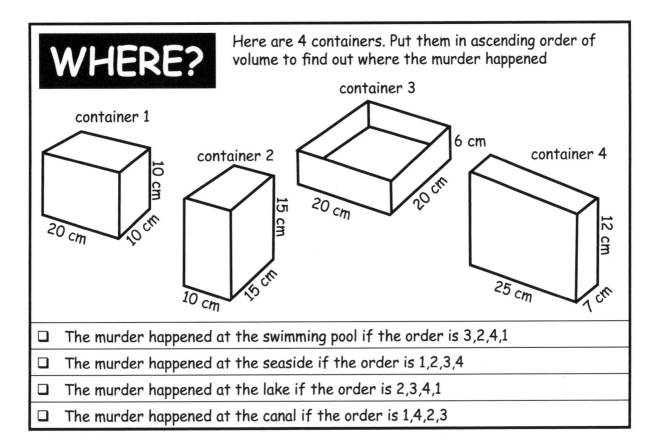

container 1 — 20 cm, 10 cm, 10 cm
container 2 — 15 cm, 10 cm, 15 cm
container 3 — 6 cm, 20 cm, 20 cm
container 4 — 12 cm, 25 cm, 7 cm

☐	The murder happened at the swimming pool if the order is 3,2,4,1
☐	The murder happened at the seaside if the order is 1,2,3,4
☐	The murder happened at the lake if the order is 2,3,4,1
☐	The murder happened at the canal if the order is 1,4,2,3

WHY?

Convert these into litres and decode the murderer's confession.

A	C	D	E	G	H	I
3600ml	1550ml	250ml	6000ml	360ml	½ litre	50ml
L	N	S	T	U	W	Z
85ml	60ml	850ml	155ml	600ml	25ml	36ml

0.5	6	0.85	3.6	0.05	0.25	0.155	0.5	6	0.85
0.6	6	0.036	1.55	3.6	0.06	3.6	0.085	0.025	3.6
0.85	0.05	0.06	6	0.06	0.36	0.085	3.6	0.06	0.25

FINAL ACCUSATION

_____ murdered _____

At (time) _____

At (where) _____

Because (why) _____

Mini Murder Mystery
Missing Pieces

WHO? The central square is missing.
The person with the correct piece is the victim.
Touching edges must match.

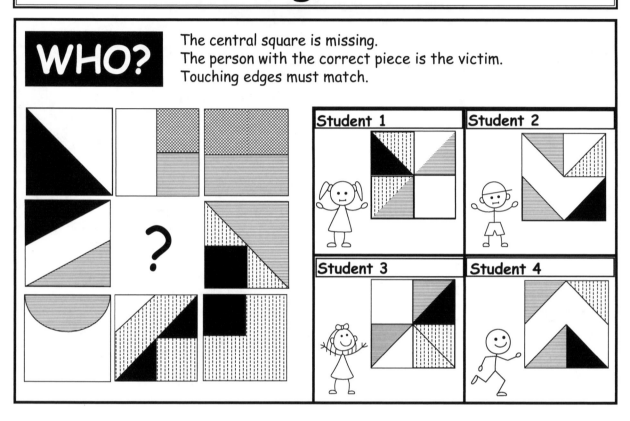

The graph below has a square missing. The murderer has the correct piece.

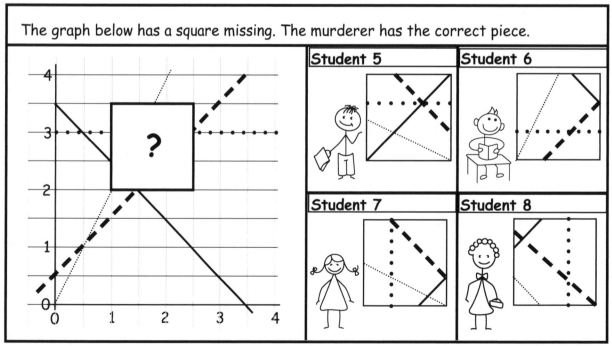

Missing Pieces – Student Sheet 1

WHEN?

One of the 4 pieces shown will fit in the maze to allow a way out.

After the holiday	In the summer holiday
At half term	Just before the end of term

WHY?

There are 4 overlapping shapes
– a rectangle, a square, a triangle and a circle.
Link the correct missing piece to the reason for the murder.

If it's A : She's very bossy	If it's B: Her face is missing	If it's C: She doesn't listen	If it's D: She took my chair away

FINAL ACCUSATION

_____ murdered _____

When _____

Because (why) _____

_____

Answers

Mystery	Who murdered whom	When	Where	Why
Mixed arithmetic 1	Joshua murdered Scarlet	9:32 on 31st Dec	Literary Festival	She said double an odd number is odd
Mixed arithmetic 2	Hercules murdered Hannah	23:57 on 19/1	Market	She said one was a prime number
Number & algebra 1	Mary Jane murdered Joshua	10:00 am	Yorkshire	He did not wear his hat
Number & algebra 2	Macey murdered Billy	16:44 on 29th Aug	Hot air balloon	He never stops talking
Number & angles	Fiona murdered Tony	Today	On the pond	He broke all the eggs
Money	Dylan murdered Elspeth	06:53 on 10th Sept	Leisure Centre	She gave me the wrong change
Coordinates	Susanna murdered Felix	10:20 on 21st Feb	(3,2)	He plotted a point in reverse
Shape	Jenny murdered Oscar	18:27	Little Lane	He said a kite had five sides
Charts	Toby murdered Fred	12:29 on 15th Oct	Pantry	He said a pea is a fruit
Family	Jill murdered Jack	3:05pm	Bottom of the hill	We went up a hill and he pushed me down
Sports	Murtada murdered Thomas	14:33 on 2nd May	Compton Rd	I wanted to win the running race
Music	Georgina murdered Benjie	30th march	Piano shop	He can't play the piano
Europe	Jack murdered Gillian	17:35 on 13th Sept	Belarus	Her name doesn't start with a J
The Romans	Juno murdered Julius	20:24 on 16th April	Leptis Magna	His month has a day more than mine
Water	Tommy murdered Brendan	5:10pm	The canal	He said the Suez Canal was in England
Missing Pieces	Jill murdered Sarah	Just before the end of term	-	She's very bossy

Answers